Changing

A KID'S VIEW OF SHELTER LIVING

MW00856183

Changing Places

A KID'S VIEW OF SHELTER LIVING

Conceived and written by
Margie Chalofsky, Glen Finland, and Judy Wallace

Illustrated by
Ingrid Klass

Designed by
Anne-Catherine Fallen
Research & Design Associates

gryphon house

Mt. Rainier, Maryland

For D. and J., wherever they may be.

© 1992 Margie Chalofsky, Glen Finland, and Judy Wallace
Published by Gryphon House, Inc.
3706 Otis Street, Mt. Rainier, Maryland 20712
Printed in the United States of America.
Library of Congress Catalog Number: 92-53893

Publisher's Cataloging in Publication
(Prepared by Quality Books, Inc.)

Chalofsky, Margery Schwartz, 1951-
     Changing places : a kid's view of shelter living / Margie Chalofsky, Judy
Wallace, Glen Finland ; illustrated by Ingrid Klass.
     p. cm.
     ISBN 0-87659-161-6
     1. Homeless children—Personal narratives. 2. Shelters for the homeless.
3. Homelessness—Personal narratives. I. Wallace, Judy Preston, 1950-
II. Finland, Glen Wilson, 1952- III. Title. IV. Title: A kid's view of shelter
living.

HV4505.C4 1992   362.73
                                        QBI92-804

DEAR READERS

The three authors of *Changing Places* met while working together at a family shelter in Virginia. We watched and were involved with children as they came in, as they claimed their new roles within the shelter and as they moved on. Often the comings and goings were marked by insecurity and fear, sadness and confusion. We were touched by the depth of feelings exhibited in behavior, though only occasionally expressed in words.

The friends in this book put words to some of those feelings. They were created to speak directly to the children we were meeting. The intent was to give the book to children as they entered our shelter. We asked the children to use the book for coloring, for writing in their own story or otherwise making it "theirs" in anyway they chose. We attempted to validate the wide range of emotions they *might* be feeling, so as not to define what they *should* be feeling. They were encouraged to share their problems with the staff and to see the shelter as a safe place, a place to help them.

The words and illustrations that create our eight friends were very carefully chosen in an effort to speak to the part of the child in crisis that feels unseen or unheard and to the child who feels very much alone. Children in the middle of family crisis often see themselves as essentially different from other children. They feel that they alone have been chosen for these burdens and that there must be something wrong with them. They may also feel responsible. We hoped this book would be one step toward breaking into that isolation.

To our great pleasure, we found that the appeal of Lamont, Bobby Nell, Anthony, Roberto, Wayne, Marcy, Ashanti and Molly is broader than we anticipated. The children in this book have deeply touched the hearts of children and adults who have listened to their stories. We invite you to enter these pages and meet our eight friends.

If you are a child who is not homeless, we hope that you like our children, that you see that they can be good friends just like you are.

If you are a parent, we hope you will use our book to teach that although all children do not share the same experiences, all children do share a common humanity and are to be treated with dignity and friendship.

If you are a teacher, you can make the difference between whether school becomes a place for a child to feel ashamed or accepted, alienated or included. We trust that through the pains and hopes of our friends, you have learned, as we have.

If you are a parent who is currently homeless, we hope this book will provide support to you and your children and will be a good way to open up discussion about your child's feelings.

If you are a child who is homeless, this book is in honor of you.

Margie Chalofsky
Glen Finland
Judy Wallace

EIGHT FRIENDS

Lamont, age 6

Bobby Nell, age 9

Anthony, age 8

Roberto, age 12

Wayne, age 13

Marcy, age 10

Ashanti, age 10

Molly, age 12

Arriving
PART I

LAMONT

"I'm Lamont. Mom and I came to this shelter late last night. I didn't know the lady asleep in the bed next to me, but Mom said I didn't need to be afraid. She said we were finally in a safe place."

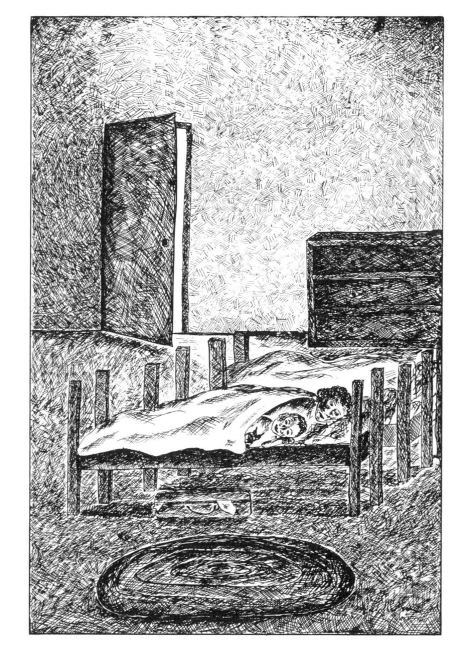

BOBBY NELL

"I'm Bobby Nell and I like the rules here. No screaming, no fighting, no drugs and no hitting. That sure beats the way things were back home...only I can't open the refrigerator whenever I want to. I don't like that part. It's not like home."

ANTHONY

"My name is Anthony. Today I have to go to court and tell the judge what Daddy did to Mom and me before we came to live here. Mom says if I tell the judge my father hurt us, he'll make Daddy stay away from us until he's better. Will I ever see him again? Will he still love me?"

ROBERTO

"My Mama doesn't speak English. Everybody is always saying, 'Roberto, tell your Mom this,' or 'What is your Mom gonna do about that...' Sometimes I get mad because I have to translate everything for Mama. Like yesterday, I wanted to go to the ball game with all the other kids, but Mama needed me to go talk to her lawyer for her. It's always somebody...the social worker, the landlord, the doctor. And the worst thing is when I have to translate over and over how mean my Daddy was to her."

WAYNE

"My name is Wayne. Mom and I got here late last night. I sure hope we get to stay for a while because this is better than where we were before. But I don't think we will. They won't let you do drugs here, and Mom uses."

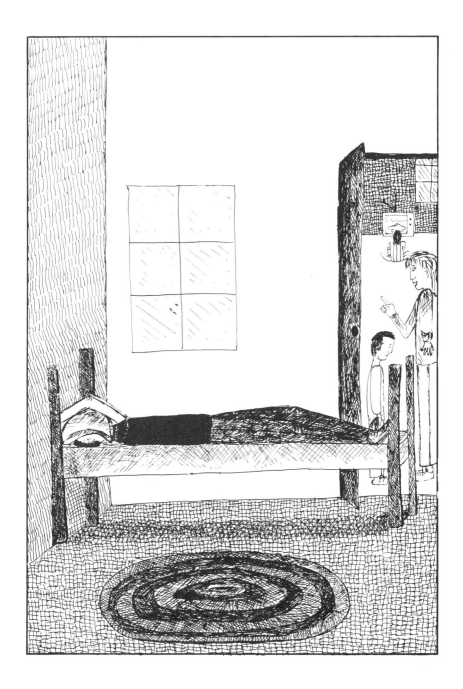

MARCY

"Hi! My name is Marcy. I like it okay here, but I've never lived with black people before. At first it seemed sort of strange, but then I met a girl the same age as me and she said she knew how I felt 'cause she'd never lived with white people. There is a boy our age here too, but we never get to play with him because his mother can't speak English, and he's always talking to somebody for her."

ASHANTI

"Marcy told you about me...I'm Ashanti, her best friend. I never had a white best friend before. Now we eat together every night. But do they have some weird food here! I just want a hotdog or something...but here we get casseroles or tuna spaghetti. You ever heard of tuna spaghetti? And there aren't any sodas. Mama says I should just be happy they give me food, but I can't figure out why I should be grateful for some gross casserole...when all I really want is a hotdog."

MOLLY

"I'm Molly Sturgil from West Virginia.
My Dad made us move here because he said
he could find work in a big city. He did get
a job, but there wasn't enough money for
a place to live. We camped in the park for
a long time, but they made us leave. So we
came to this shelter, and it's pretty nice. I
heard a lady who works here tell Mom we
could stay in another shelter while we saved
money for our own place. Mom's going
over there tomorrow. I hope we get in."

Staying
PART II

LAMONT

"Sunday is Mother's Day, and my Mom is the best Mom in the whole wide world. I wanted to buy her a house. She could cook pancakes and hotdogs for me all day long. Last night a volunteer helped me draw a picture of Mom in her new house. I think she'll like my picture 'cause it's from me."

BOBBY NELL

"I had a lot of friends at my old school, but now I'm in a school where nobody knows me. I'm always left out because I'm new here. One girl asked me where I lived, but I didn't tell her. I got scared she'd think 'cause we're homeless that Mom's lazy or doesn't take care of us. But that's not true. My Mom wants to work again. She's trying hard to get another job."

ANTHONY

"When we first came here I was really mad at Dad for hitting Mom. He does it all the time. But now I want to go home. I keep telling Mom that if we go home now Dad will be so glad to see us that he'll never hit her again. Mom says, 'Don't forget, he always promises not to hit me...but he hasn't stopped yet.' "

ROBERTO

"I made Mama cry today, and I feel bad.
I just had to tell her I needed new shoes
'cause my sneakers had holes in them. She
started crying and said she couldn't take care
of me. I didn't mean to get her that
upset...then a lady who works here saw
Mama crying and asked me why. She said,
'You know, that's one problem I think we
can solve right here, right now.' Then she
came out of the office with a nearly new pair
of sneakers...my size!...and said, 'Roberto,
tell your Mama that being a good mother
is about loving and not about money for
sneakers.' "

WAYNE

"I got in a fight with another kid at the shelter today. He took my football, and when I told him to give it back to me, he just laughed. I was so mad I could've smashed him. People I didn't even know were yelling at me, but Mom acted like she didn't even hear anything. She's so worried about her own problems, she ignores me now. But that's okay, I've always had to take care of myself."

MARCY & ASHANTI

"Hey, Marcy...I've been thinking. If we could talk our mothers into sharing a place to live, then it would only be half as hard for them to come up with the rent money every month...and we'd still be together. Any chance your mother might do it?"

"I don't know, Ashanti. My Mom's kinda funny about living with strangers. 'Course, I keep telling her, nothing's stranger than the guy she used to live with. Let me see what she says..."

MOLLY

"Dad keeps saying that Sturgils don't take charity; they never have and they never will. He wants us to get out of this shelter, but there is nowhere to go, except back home, and there is no work there. Even the mines are closed. He says he'd rather we slept in the truck. I'm not sure what charity is, but it sure beats sleeping in the truck."

Moving On
PART III

LAMONT

"You know...there were lots of people here who helped me and Mom find a place of our own. Well, not really our own. We'll be sharing an apartment, but we can stay there for three whole months. We leave here first thing in the morning, but you know...I remember at first I was afraid to come, but now I might even miss some of the people here. It was okay being here."

BOBBY NELL

"My Mama says she's taking us back south to live with family. She thinks she can get a job at the mill 'cause she's union and everything. I hope I can get my friends back that easy. But, you know...here, the kids were starting to be kind of nice. One even asked me to come play at her house sometime. So I guess I'll be starting over again, too."

ANTHONY

"I talked to a lady who works here about how much I want to go back to Daddy. She says lots of kids feel that way. She says it's okay to love Daddy and miss him, but right now, the most important thing is that Mom and I are safe. That's cool. I thought I was supposed to hate him...but sometimes I don't."

ROBERTO

"Guess what! Mama and I stopped at this Mexican restaurant yesterday to use the phone, and while I was translating all the stuff for her lawyer...she talked the owner into a job! She's gonna cook enchiladas and fajitas for pay...and my Mama loves to cook! ALL RIGHT, MAMA!"

WAYNE

"The staff's been talking to Mom about some treatment maybe she could go to for, you know, her problems with drugs and stuff. I don't know where we're going from here, but Mom says we're leaving. She just can't stop using."

MARCY & ASHANTI

"WE DID IT, ASHANTI! WE DID IT! WE DID IT! When the social worker found a two bedroom apartment, Mom said she'd take it if she could split the rent with somebody. And Ashanti's Mom was standing right there when she said it. I looked up at Mrs. Johnson and said, 'PUH-LEEZE come with us?' Mrs. Johnson just laughed and said, 'We'll see.' "

"Well, we went to see it the next afternoon, and—this is so cool— at the end of the month, we're all moving in together. I mean, it's really gonna happen!"

MOLLY

"You know, my dad's right. Sturgils won't take no hand-outs. He misses the mountains, and I guess there are worse things out there than sleepin' in the truck at the county park. But while we were here, the way these people tried to help us and all...That sure did feel like the next closest thing to family. Yep...it sure felt safe."

TO PARENTS AND OTHER ADULTS

Now that you have met these eight families, we hope that you have a clearer understanding of the problems facing people in shelters. We also hope we have inspired you with a desire to help. There are many simple ways you can make a difference. Contact your local shelter, social service or any group in your area that assists the homeless. Tell them how much time, energy or money you would like to invest and ask them what they need most. Small donations of food, warm clothes or personal care items can make a big difference. On a larger scale, organize a group project, such as collecting money for a family to use as the security deposit on an apartment. Be creative and think of your own skills. If you are computer literate, compose resumes. If you are a doctor, offer a free office visit. If you are a warm person, offer to be a friend. There are numerous ways you can help and you will get back more than you give. You can make a difference.

TO ALL CHILDREN

We found that children are valuable friends to the homeless. Classes and scout troops can do wonderful things when they put their minds to it. They can cook meals and cookies, clean up, donate toys and organize food drives. Children and young people are great helpers, and we found that you were always ready to help. Think about what you can do to help others and don't forget that someone you know may be in a shelter. If you have a classmate who is in a shelter, welcome her/him with an extra smile and ask her/him to join in whatever game you are playing. Being in a shelter can be a lonely experience, and your being a friend means a lot. You really can help make a difference.